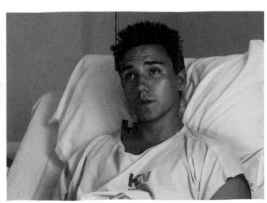

SHARKWATER ™

Library and Archives Canada Cataloguing in Publication

Stewart, Rob, 1979–

    Sharkwater : based on the award-winning documentary / Rob Stewart.

ISBN-13: 978-1-55263-971-9 , ISBN-10: 1-55263-971-1

    1. Sharks. 2. Sharks--Effect of human beings on. I. Title.

QL638.9.S76 2007   597.3   C2007-904420-4

ONTARIO ARTS COUNCIL
CONSEIL DES ARTS DE L'ONTARIO

The publisher gratefully acknowledges the support of the Canada Council for the Arts and the Ontario Arts Council for its publishing program. We acknowledge the support of the Government of Ontario through the Ontario Media Development Corporation's Ontario Book Initiative.

We acknowledge the financial support of the Government of Canada through the Book Publishing Industry Development Program (BPIDP) for our publishing activities.

Key Porter Books Limited
Six Adelaide Street East, Tenth Floor
Toronto, Ontario
Canada M5C 1H6

www.keyporter.com

Design: Marijke Friesen

Printed and bound in Canada

07 08 09 10 11 5 4 3 2 1

SHARKWATER™

ROB STEWART

KEY PORTER BOOKS

TABLE OF CONTENTS

Scalloped hammerhead shark, Cocos Island, Costa Rica. Hammerheads are incredibly sensitive sharks. Their heads are giant sensory systems that detect magnetic fields through sensors called ampullae of Lorenzini. These huge heads can sense the magnetic field of a hidden fish, allowing the shark to hone in on its heartbeat, and find food buried in sand or hidden in rocks. They can also use the earth's magnetic field to follow undersea ridges like roadmaps, navigating thousands of miles through the oceans.

Shovelnose ray, *Yongala* wreck, Queensland, Australia. Shovelnose rays, despite looking like sharks, are actually rays. Sharks breathe in through their mouths, which are at the front of their bodies, and out through their gills, located on the sides of their bodies. Rays spend a lot of time living and feeding on the sea floor, so their mouths and gills are located on the underside of their bodies. To take in water to breathe, they also have holes on the top of their heads called spiracles.

Schooling scalloped hammerhead sharks, Wolf Island, Galápagos Islands, Ecuador. Hammerheads are one of the most recently evolved shark species, having evolved only 70 million years ago. We know very little about sharks, including where most species mate, give birth or how long they live. A new species of hammerhead shark that can grow 12 feet long was just discovered in the Caribbean in 2006, and more new species of sharks are discovered every year.

ABOVE: **A hook from the first longlines I encountered at Darwin Island, Galápagos, Ecuador.** We pulled up thousands of hooks that day, many of which had hooked sharks, manta rays, tuna and billfish. Hooks used to rust and fall out of fish, but stronger metals and stainless steel make the hooks stronger and less likely to rust and degrade.

LEFT: **Silvertip shark trailing hook and metal leader, Cocos Island, Costa Rica.** Silvertip sharks are heavy-bodied sharks that are known to consume other sharks. This juvenile was a lucky survivor from an encounter with a long-liner or fisherman, but it will trail the hook and leader for a long time.

Me freediving in the Similan Islands, Thailand. Freediving was my introduction to the underwater world. When I was too young to scuba dive, holding my breath and swimming down was the only way to get close to fish. It became a passion of mine, and came in handy while filming *Sharkwater* as many animals such as sharks, whales, and dolphins do not like scuba equipment and bubbles, and are far easier to approach while freediving.
PHOTO: TERRA MACK

FOREWORD

"ELEPHANTS KILL MORE PEOPLE EACH YEAR THAN SHARKS DO, SO THERE'S SOME DEEP-SEATED PSYCHOLOGICAL REVULSION ABOUT A COLD-EYED MONSTER COMING OUT OF THE DEEP AND PICKING YOU TO PIECES, BUT THAT IS THE MYTH, NOT THE REALITY."
—DR. SAMUEL GRUBER, SHARK BIOLOGIST

When I set out to make the film *Sharkwater*, I was a naïve 22-year-old wildlife photographer and biologist who wanted to help sharks. I discovered that sharks were being decimated, and that the world was completely unaware, largely because the world was afraid of sharks. I spent enough time with sharks as a child and as a photographer to know that my perception of them was very different from the public's *Jaws*-based impression that sharks were menacing predators of people.

Sharks are at the top of the ocean's ecosystem, existing in balance with an underwater world that has hosted life for billions of years. Sharks are incredibly sophisticated and adaptable animals with senses not found in land creatures, making sharks capable of surviving whatever natural hardships the earth throws at them. They've even survived five major extinctions when over 90 percent of species were wiped out.

Life on earth evolved in the oceans. As phytoplankton (tiny plants) in the oceans evolved, they started sequestering carbon dioxide and releasing oxygen. The planet cooled, the atmosphere became hospitable for terrestrial life, and life evolved on land. Teeming with life, the oceans continue to support life on the surface, generating 70 percent of the oxygen we breathe. Considering that phytoplankton in the oceans are the largest consumers of carbon dioxide, the greenhouse gas that is causing global warming, it's clear we can't think about global warming without considering the oceans. Sharks sit at the top of oceanic ecosystems, controlling populations of animals below them, including phytoplankton, making sharks crucial to the balance of both terrestrial and aquatic life on earth. Sharks are species that deserve protection.

In April 2002, I set out to make a beautiful underwater film that brought people closer to sharks than ever before. I wanted to show the reality of a beautiful creature so perfectly adapted to life on earth that it has survived longer than any other large animal. I believed if I could show the reality that sharks want very little to do with humans then the public might be moved to fight for their protection, as they do for pandas, elephants and bears.

Having never shot footage with a video camera before, I was banking on my ability to take pretty still pictures underwater and translate that skill into making pretty underwater motion pictures.

My simple mission of creating a beautiful underwater film became immensely complicated when, three weeks into shooting, we were forced to gather evidence in our own defense by filming *ourselves*, to

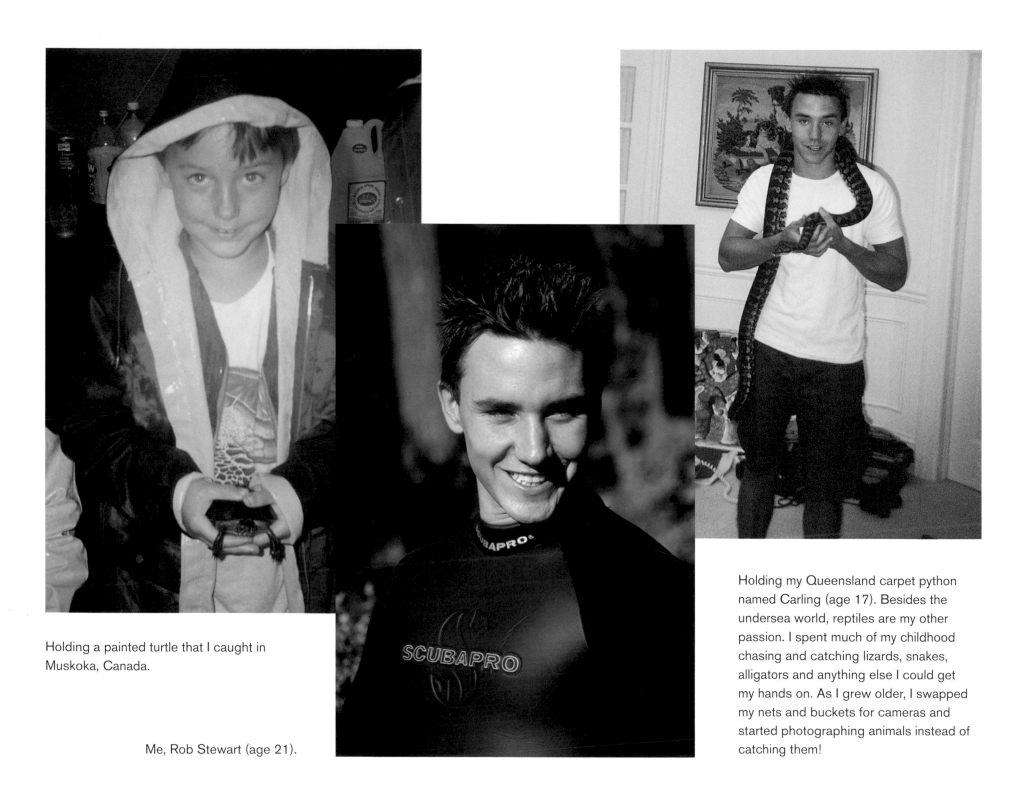

Holding a painted turtle that I caught in Muskoka, Canada.

Me, Rob Stewart (age 21).

Holding my Queensland carpet python named Carling (age 17). Besides the undersea world, reptiles are my other passion. I spent much of my childhood chasing and catching lizards, snakes, alligators and anything else I could get my hands on. As I grew older, I swapped my nets and buckets for cameras and started photographing animals instead of catching them!

keep *ourselves* out of prison. That story of pirate boat rammings, corrupt governments, mafia and coast guard chases, espionage, hospitalizations and the exploitation of the oceans behind it all resulted in the film *Sharkwater*, and the book you are now holding in your hands. The intertwined lives of sharks and man, and the human drama that unfolded in the film forced me to become a serious filmmaker, taking on a five-year,

15-country journey that would nearly end my life, and most definitely, change it forever.

Sharkwater is not just a film about saving sharks. It is about saving the oceans, and ultimately about saving humanity. The earth and its residents have been here for billions of years. We're the newcomers, and it's our survival that's in jeopardy.

Douglas Braun and me photographing colobus
monkeys in Kenya.

While I was finishing university in Kenya, I met
Lena, from Turkana, while my school program
was visiting her village. I was the first white
person she met, and she was so excited to see
me that she spent the day holding my hands and
walking around on my feet. PHOTO: TERRA MACK

Here I'm teaching Jay Rhind and Tyler Schlodnick
how to dive. They are now studying marine biology
at Queens University. I started teaching scuba
so I could introduce people to the underwater
world. I always preferred teaching kids.

Sea lions and sleeping lions rock, Galápagos Islands, Ecuador. Sea lions have evolved hyper mobile backbones that make them extremely agile in the water, and a challenging target for sharks. For sharks to catch sea lions, they have to ambush them or find an injured one flapping around on the surface of the water. An injured sea lion on the surface looks and sounds much like a swimming human would, yet so few people are bitten each year, which is a huge testament to sharks' sensory systems.

THE GALÁPAGOS ISLANDS

"WHAT I BELIEVE IS THAT THE WHOLE PLANET WAS LIKE THIS. I THINK ANIMALS WERE AMAZINGLY ABUNDANT;
I THINK WHALES WERE AMAZINGLY ABUNDANT, FISH WERE AMAZINGLY ABUNDANT, TURTLES, BIRDS, EVERYTHING,
BEFORE MAN GOT IN THERE AND REALLY HACKED THE WHOLE THING TO PIECES."
—GODFREY MERLIN, GALÁPAGOS NATIONAL PARK/WILDAID

I've loved sharks ever since I was a child. I grew up filling aquariums with predators, and spent much of my time scouring the underwater world for new creatures and looking for sharks.

In July 2000, I was 19 years old and on my first assignment to photograph hammerhead sharks—one of my favorites. I spent two days getting to the Galápagos Islands, a remote archipelago which lies 600 miles off the coast of Ecuador in the middle of the Pacific.

The Galápagos Islands is one of the most isolated places on earth, and is the inspiration for Charles Darwin's theory of evolution that revolutionized global thought. Prior to Darwin's work, the general consensus was that the earth was created by God in seven days, and that all creatures were created as they appear today. Darwin's evolutionary theory spoke to species' ability to adapt and change over time, and that the species we have today have evolved from others.

Life in the Galápagos is absolutely unique. Many animals, such as the marine iguana and blue-footed booby are endemic—occurring nowhere else on earth. There are no large terrestrial predators in the Galápagos, so the wildlife has not learned to fear large animals. Most can be easily approached closely by humans.

After photographing the diverse life on land, I traveled 160 miles from the center of the Galápagos to Darwin and Wolf islands, two remote undersea volcanoes that barely break the ocean surface, and two of the few places on earth where hammerhead sharks congregate in schools. Hammerheads are a recent evolutionary experiment—only 70 million years old. Much of the sharks' sensory systems are located on the underside of their snouts—giving hammerheads an increased surface area for their sensory systems. Their heads also make them extremely agile in the water.

Currents converge in the Galápagos from Antarctica, the Americas, and the Pacific, causing nutrient-rich waters to collide with the base of the islands deep in the sea and well up to the surface. This allows plankton to bloom in huge quantities, making the Galápagos an area of very high productivity, supporting huge numbers of large predators—sharks, tunas, billfish, and cetaceans (dolphins, whales and porpoises). The Galápagos is one of the only areas on the planet where sharks are protected, and they school there in the thousands, socializing and mating.

When we arrived at Darwin Island, instead of finding hammerheads in all their majesty underwater, I found hundreds of sharks dead and

Marine iguana feeding on algae, Fernandina Island, Galápagos Islands, Ecuador.
Marine iguanas are the only seagoing lizard in the world. They use their huge claws to hold onto rocks in the surge while they feed on algae growing in the rich and cold waters of the Galápagos.

dying on a longline that was 60 miles long; long enough to stretch from earth to outer space. A longline is a fishing line that floats along the surface of the water, with as many as 16,000 baited hooks descending into the water at a predetermined depth. Longline fishing is indiscriminate, hooking sharks, tunas, billfish, sea turtles, sea lions, sea birds, and other large marine animals swimming near the surface. Fishermen are usually only interested in a few species, and the rest are discarded.

I was on board the *Aggressor*, a live-aboard diving ship that takes tourists diving with sharks. Sixteen of us planned on diving with schooling hammerhead sharks. But instead of diving with sharks, the crew and paying passengers spent the day pulling in the longlines and releasing the sharks that were still alive. I photographed and filmed the incident, in hopes of giving the evidence to the authorities so the boat could be prosecuted. I soon learned that not only would the boat go free, but finding longlines in the Galápagos was extremely common due to intense foreign and local fishing pressure, much of which was illegal.

Ecuador is pro-conservation, and the Galápagos Islands is surrounded by one of the largest marine reserves on earth, designed to protect the region's unique marine habitat and keep the tourism industry alive. Much of Ecuador's income comes from tourism in the Galápagos, but local and foreign fishermen have realized the immense value of its underwater resources, and pressure to raise fishing quotas has increased exponentially. The conflict between fishermen and the tourism industry has resulted in fishermen rioting, burning bridges and threatening national park staff. The head of the national park was rescued by the navy while he was hiding from fishermen in a mangrove forest. Violence in the Galápagos has traditionally worked for fishermen, resulting in increased or removed fishing quotas.

It made no sense to me why sharks were being killed in one of the most protected areas on the planet, in a national park that is also a UNESCO World Heritage Site. I needed to know why people were killing sharks, so I embarked on a journey around the world, to photograph them and their ecosystems, and get to the bottom of the issue.

Cactus and lava scenic, Galápagos Islands, Ecuador.
Many of the terrestrial ecosystems in the Galápagos are very dry, desert-like environments, without much rainfall. The arid environment means that many of the land animals are dependent on the oceans for food, returning to the sea to feed daily.

Sally lightfoot crab, Esmeralda Island, Galápagos Islands, Ecuador.
These crabs can be as large as eight inches wide, and are found throughout
the Galápagos. They're deathly afraid of the water and are named "lightfoot"
for their ability to nearly fly over tide pools.

Marine Iguana holding rock in crashing waves, North Seymour Island, Galápagos Islands, Ecuador. These iguanas are incredibly strong, able to hold on to rocks with their huge claws, even in waves that sent me flying. I photographed this iguana using a slow shutter speed to show the movement of the water in contrast to the still iguana.

Blue-footed booby and chick, North Seymour Island, Galápagos Islands, Ecuador. Blue-footed boobies flirt with their bright blue feet, which are used for sexual selection. The brighter the feet, the better the mate. In mating season they spend hours showing each other their feet, in hopes of attracting a mate. The fuzzy white chicks depend on regurgitated fish from the parents, who take turns venturing out to sea. There are no large predators in the Galápagos, so boobies are not afraid of humans, and are easily approached.

Flightless cormorant drying rudimentary wings, Fernandina Island, Galápagos Islands, Ecuador. Cormorants are excellent swimmers and use their huge feet and long necks to catch fish underwater. All other cormorants dry their wings and feathers after swimming so they can fly. Flightless cormorants lost their ability to fly because there were no large predators in the Galápagos, and flight was no longer necessary, but they still dry their rudimentary wings in the sun!

Frigate bird, Galápagos Islands, Ecuador. Frigates are aerial acrobats. They often steal the food of other seabirds instead of catching their own. They also torment birds in mid-air so much that they regurgitate recently consumed fish, which the frigates intercept as they fall.

FACING PAGE: **Frigate male displaying its red gular sac, North Seymour Island, Galápagos Islands, Ecuador.** Male frigates have huge gular sacs, which they inflate during mating season to attract mates. Every time a female flies overhead, the male will shake his gular sac and emit a chatter to attract her.

Finding 60 miles of illegally set longlines at Darwin Island, Galápagos, an Ecuadorian national park, UNESCO World Heritage Site, and one of the seven underwater wonders of the world, was a huge surprise for me, opening my eyes to just how valuable sharks are. I arrived eager and expecting to photograph these amazing creatures in one of the last sanctuaries for sharks on the planet. I left with a mission to educate the public about the sharks' plight.

The crew and passengers spent the day pulling in and releasing over 160 sharks, manta rays, and a few tuna and sailfish. The illegal fishing boats fled and were never caught, just like innumerable other poachers in the Galápagos. The Ecuadorian Navy is in charge of protecting the marine reserve, though they have very few patrol boats to police the huge marine reserve. Poachers were raiding the Galápagos every day.

LEFT: The eight-hour affair exhausted the crew and passengers, and wore through two dive knives and 13 gloves. Longlines can have more than 16,000 baited hooks that ensnare sharks, billfish, tuna, sea lions, sea turtles and sea birds.

FACING PAGE: An *Aggressor* crewmember cutting a Galápagos shark free. The sharks were being fished for their fins, to make shark fin soup, a delicacy in much of Asia. The high cost of the soup has led to finning, where fishermen keep only the fins, and discard the bodies, wasting 95 percent of the animal.

BOTTOM: This sailfish suffocated, as it wrapped itself up in the line while struggling to free itself.

A coral trout and soft coral, Similan Islands, Thailand.
Life evolved in the seas and eventually moved onto land. The oceans contain billions of years of evolutionary complexity that humans are only beginning to understand. When compared to the hundreds of millions of years life has been evolving on land, it's easy to see why the oceans need protection.

SHARKS AND THEIR ECOSYSTEMS

"THE KILLING OF SHARKS IS THE BIGGEST ECOLOGICAL TIME BOMB WE'RE GOING TO FACE PRETTY SOON. WE HAVE TO UNDERSTAND THAT SHARKS ARE THE MOST ABUNDANT TOP PREDATOR ON THIS PLANET OVER 100 POUNDS, SO THAT TELLS YOU SOMETHING. NATURE CREATED THEM FOR A REASON. NOW HUMAN BEINGS, THEY DON'T CARE IF WE KILL 100 MILLION, [IF] WE KILL 200 MILLION, SO WHAT? YOU KNOW? THAT SHARK'S A NUISANCE, THAT SHARK IS A GOOD SHARK, LET'S KILL THEM ALL. BUT IF WE KILL THEM ALL, WE DESTROY ALL FOOD CHAINS OF AN ENTIRE MARINE ECOSYSTEM AND WELL, THE MAJORITY OF OUR OXYGEN COMES FROM THE OCEAN, SO WE SHOULD BE MORE CAREFUL." —DR. ERICH RITTER, SHARK BIOLOGIST

Sharks are among the most unique animals on the planet.

Sharks were among the first vertebrates with jaws, evolving when there was very little life on land—when the planet's earth mass comprised only two continents. Sharks have shown themselves to be extremely adaptable, existing in every ocean on earth except the Antarctic sea. They live under arctic ice, and in the darkest depths of the oceans.

They range in size from the 7-inch (20-cm) dwarf lanternshark to the 50-foot (15-m) whale shark—the world's largest fish. Sharks are cartilaginous animals called elasmobranchs, belonging to the group of Chondrichthyes, which contains sharks, skates, rays, and chimeras. Unlike bony fish, sharks have no swim bladders for buoyancy and therefore will sink when not swimming. Sharks have rows of conveyor-like teeth that are replaced throughout their lifetime, and it's no surprise that shark teeth are the most commonly found fossils.

Because sharks have been on the planet for such a long time, they have evolved to dominate the undersea ecosystem, shaping life in the oceans. As the top predator, they impact the species lower in the food chain, and provide a framework for ocean life. Their influence in oceanic food chains is felt as far down as the phytoplankton, that provides 70 percent of the oxygen we breathe.

Sharks are essential for life in the seas.

I traveled the world photographing sharks and their ecosystems by every continent they're found, trying to find out why shark populations were plummeting. I discovered shark populations had declined as much as 90 percent in the last 30 years. Some species such as the oceanic whitetip shark, once the most abundant large predator on the planet, had declined 99 percent in the Gulf of Mexico.

This is due to the demand for fins. Shark fin soup is a symbol of wealth and respect through much of Asia, particularly China and Hong Kong. It has become a ubiquitous dish at weddings, banquets and business dinners, fetching as much as $200 a bowl. A single pound of fin is worth over $300. Sharks meant money, and they were being killed in every country with a coastline. Sharks have low reproductive rates, giving birth to mostly live young, producing very few pups, and taking up to 25 years to reach sexual maturity, with gestation periods of up to three years. Sharks are apex predators, and in over 400 million years, have never evolved to be preyed upon with such force. Sharks were being wiped out at a rate of 100 million a year, and nobody knew about it.

I needed to make a film so that I could bring this issue to the masses.

Schooling chevron barracuda, Sipadan Island, Malaysian Borneo. Barracuda are often erroneously thought of as dangerous sea creatures, but as you can see in this picture, you can be amongst thousands of them without a problem. Barracuda are often trained to take food from the hand, and sometimes mistake jewelry for the shining sides of a fish in a hand. They actually have very few conical-shaped teeth that are ineffective cutting tools, which is why they mostly eat things they can swallow whole, human beings not being one of them.

Linecheeked wrasse, Coral Sea, Australia. These wrasse provided a great deal of humor while filming on the Great Barrier Reef. There were always one or two of them hanging out curiously watching us underwater and they ended up in nearly every shot we have of a reef!

FACING PAGE: **Clark's anemonefish, Lankayan Island, Malaysian Borneo.** Anemonefish live amongst venomous anemones by secreting a protective layer that blocks the sting. The anemones serve as protection from predators, so anemonefish rarely leave the anemone for long.

Gorgonian wrapper anemone, Kapalai Island, Malaysian Borneo. These anemones only emerge at night. By day they look like hard coral, but at night, the animal emerges with all arms ready and willing to ensnare passing plankton.

Crocodile fish eyes, Kapalai Island, Malaysian Borneo. Crocodile fish are amazing animals. They can grow up to 4 feet long, and are well camouflaged. They are ambush predators, lying in wait for their next meal to stumble upon them.

Batfish, Sipadan Island, Malaysian Borneo.

Clown anemonefish, Myanmar. Anemonefish, and in particular clownfish, or "Nemos" as they're now referred to in Australia, became incredibly popular in the pet trade after the film *Finding Nemo* was released, and they were virtually wiped off the Great Barrier Reef. Unfortunately, some children who wanted to "set Nemo free," flushed them down the toilet.

FACING PAGE: **Clark's anemonefish,** *Yongala* **wreck, Queensland, Australia.**

White-eyed moray eel, Myanmar. Moray eels are thought by some to be dangerous, which is a misconception. Morays open and close their mouths to breathe, making them look more menacing than they are.

Mating coral trout and glassy sweepers, *Yongala* **wreck, Queensland, Australia.**

Whip goby and sea fan, Layang Layang, Malaysian Borneo. The oceans were once teeming with life, with ecosystems built upon other living creatures, such as this goby living on a sea fan, and a further myriad of life living on the goby. Fishing methods that we currently use waste 54 billion pounds of fish each year. Bottom trawling, for example, drags huge weighted nets along the sea floor, scooping up every animal and ecosystem in its path. Without the living structures on the sea floor to support ecosystems, fisheries often don't recover.

Porcelain crab, Sipadan Islands, Thailand. Porcelain crabs live on the underside of sea anemones in a symbiotic relationship. The crab benefits from the protection of the anemone, but the anemone doesn't appear to benefit from the relationship.

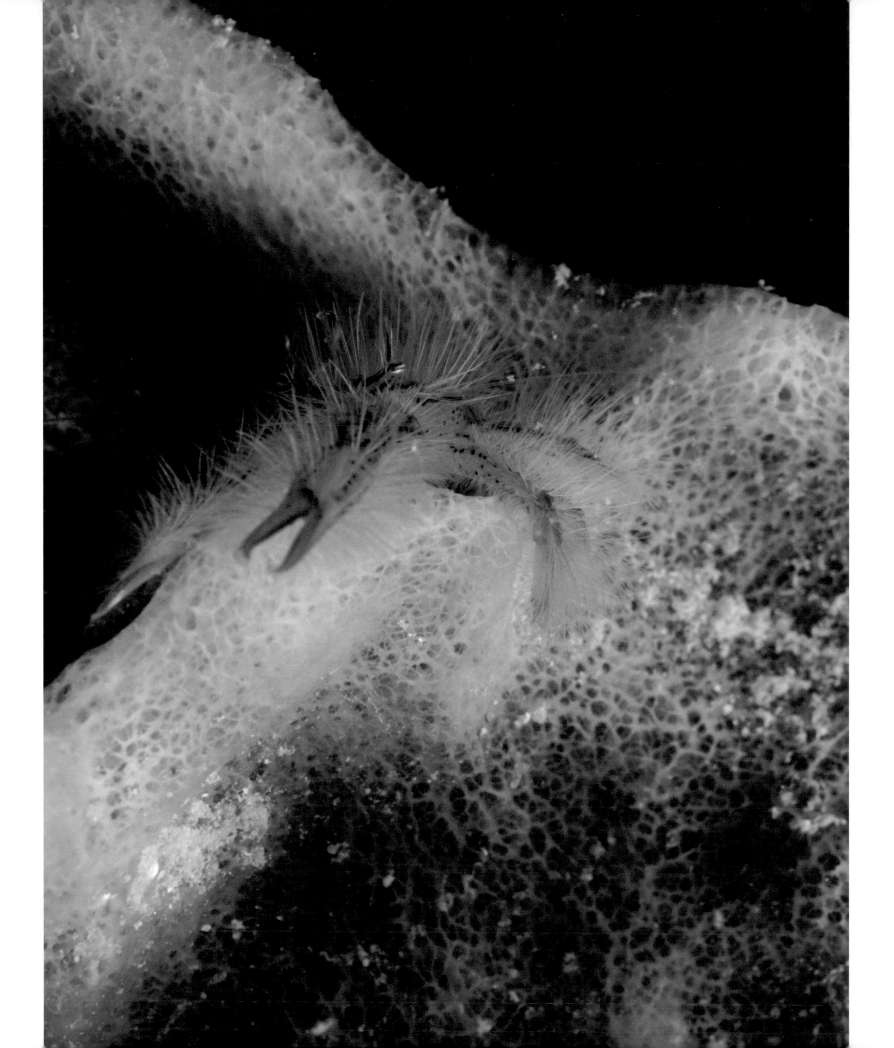

Commensal crabs living on the skin of a sea cucumber, Kapalai Island, Malaysian Borneo. This colony of crabs may spend their entire lives living on and sometimes inside a sea cucumber.

FACING PAGE: **A hairy squat lobster, Sangalaki Island, Indonesia.** Hairy squat lobsters are about 1 inch (2.5 cm) long, and hide out in crevices on sponges and soft coral. They look like crabs, but are actually small lobsters.

A sabertooth blenny peering out from coral, Sangalaki Island, Indonesia. Sabertooth blennies look like cleaner fish, so large fish approach them to have parasites removed. When the large fish are close enough, the sabertooth blenny swims up and bites off a chunk of flesh, then retreats into its hole.

FACING PAGE: **A brittle star on soft coral, Sipadan Island, Malaysian Borneo.**

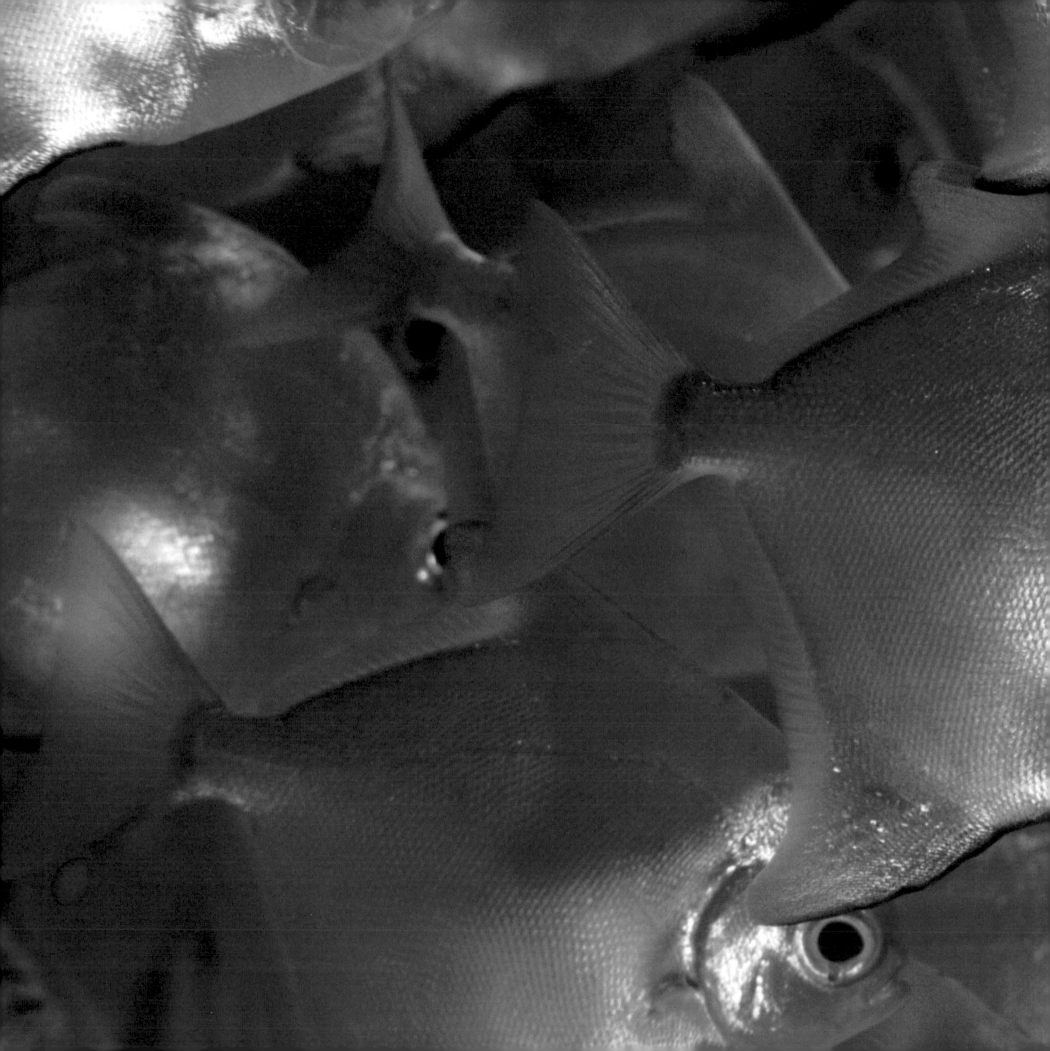

Endangered West Indian manatee, Crystal River, Florida. Manatees are slow moving mammals that feed off of vegetation in both freshwater rivers and in the ocean, and are often referred to as sea cows. They grow to 12 feet (4 m) in length and 2,000 pounds (907 kg). They are often killed by fast-moving boats and now there are only a few thousand left, mostly in the state of Florida.

PREVIOUS PAGES: **Schooling batfish, Nosy Be, Madagascar.** Many fish form schools to minimize their chances of being singled out by a predator.

Mating pharaoh cuttlefish, Burma Banks, Myanmar.
These cuttlefish are displaying mating behavior. The large one in the center is the male, guarding the smaller female cuttlefish below from the advances of a small sneaker male above. Sneaker males are genetically different than normal large males. Their strategy is to avoid aggression from the large males by looking like a female, and sneaking in to mate.

Porcelain crab, Nosy Be, northern Madagascar. I found this porcelain crab on a very murky dive in Nosy Be. Out of the murk, I saw this glowing pink light coming from the sand. I swam over and found this porcelain crab filter feeding in a glowing pink anemone. It was such a spectacular sight, I photographed it with three different kids of film in hopes of capturing the glowing pink color. None of the films captured just how bright and beautiful the scene was.

A tigertail seahorse, Nosy Be, Madagascar. This seahorse was quite shy, taking a long time to warm up and look at me allowing me to photograph it.

Blue ribbon eel, Kapalai Island, Malaysian Borneo. Bright colors in the terrestrial world often indicate that the animal is poisonous or toxic. It serves as a warning for predators to stay away. Underwater, almost everything is brightly colored.

Coral scene, Bay Islands, Honduras. Coral reef systems are some of the most biodiverse ecosystems on earth, containing as many species as a tropical rainforest. A reef in the Caribbean can have 500 different species, whereas a coral reef in Papua New Guinea, closer to where coral reefs evolved, can have over 3,000 different species.

Orange cup coral, Watamu, Kenya. Orange cup coral only comes out at night to reveal its beautiful orange arms, which help it to feed off plankton. Colonies of orange cup coral can be the size of large floor rugs.

Schooling scalloped hammerhead sharks, Cocos Island, Costa Rica.
Scalloped hammerhead sharks, unlike other hammerheads, are known to congregate at seamounts or remote islands in schools that number in the hundreds. The schools are mostly female, with the largest females vying for position in the center of the school, where males come to choose mates. Females use aggressive displays to deter smaller females.

Whale shark and divers, Darwin Island, Galápagos. Whale sharks were one of the first shark species to be listed on the Convention on International Trade in Endangered Species (CITES), along with the great white and basking sharks. The first fish was listed on CITES only in 2004, a testament to how difficult it is to get protection for marine species. Even now, only the largest and most charismatic, not necessarily the most endangered species are listed.

Diver and school of jacks (trevally), Sipadan Island, Malaysian Borneo. Scuba diving is like exploring another universe. Humans have explored more of the surface of the moon than we have of the sea floor. The sea is truly the last frontier, home to species, senses, and systems that land has never seen. It's also incredibly easy to learn to dive, and underwater you get to fly!

Nurse Shark, Bay Islands, Honduras. Nurse sharks, along with wobbegongs can lie on the seafloor, and don't have to continuously swim to breathe. They breathe by opening and closing their mouths to force water over their gills. Nurse sharks are often seen in the pet trade, despite growing to more than 12 feet long and 300 pounds!

FACING PAGE: **Olive sea snake, *Yongala* wreck, Queensland, Australia.** Sea snakes are rear fanged snakes. Unlike traditional venomous snakes like cobras and rattlesnakes, their fangs are in the back of their mouths, making it difficult for them to inject venom into something that isn't already in their mouths. They're actually quite docile, but are some of the most venomous creatures on the planet, and should be treated with respect.

Manta ray, Sangalaki Island, Indonesia. Manta rays are cartilaginous animals called elasmobranchs, belonging to the group of Chondrichthyes, which contains sharks, skates, rays, and chimeras. Mantas are the largest ray, estimated to grow to more than 21 feet from tip to tip. They are filter feeders, like whale sharks, filtering tiny plankton from the water.

Tassled wobbegong shark, Byron Bay, South Australia. Wobbegongs are incredibly camouflaged sharks. They're perfectly adapted to lying on the seafloor in wait of their next meal. They're particularly fond of octopus and lobster, which they crush up with their molar-like teeth.

Jacks (trevally), *Yongala* **wreck, Queensland, Australia.** Advanced fishing technologies, including sonar and spotter planes have increased fishing efficiency so much so that every single fishery is estimated to entirely collapse by the year 2048.

PREVIOUS PAGES: Left: **Coral trout,** *Yongala* **wreck, Queensland, Australia.**
Right: **Yellow damselfish and sweepers, Thailand.** When settlers first arrived in North America they spoke of seas so rich in fish that you could walk from the ship to shore on the backs of the fish. We've now seen the effects of over-fishing, as 90 per cent of the ocean's large predators are now gone.

Goby with eggs, Kapalai Island, Malaysian Borneo. Gobies keep their eggs in their mouths for months while they mature. The goby will swish them around sometimes spitting them out and sucking them back in again to aerate them. They eventually hatch and are released from the goby's mouth, with a far greater survival rate because of the parental care.

Lion's mane jellyfish, _Yongala_ wreck, Queensland Australia. The _Yongala_ wreck lies in 90 feet of water, 48 miles off the coast of Townsville, in Queensland, Australia. It was a steel- and- timber steamship that sank during a cyclone almost 100 years ago, taking the lives of all 121 passengers. It is one of the only structures in the channel where it lies, so much of the life in the area congregates there.

Coral scene, Lankayan Island, Malaysian Borneo. A coral reef system from the "bio-diverse triangle," the area between Papua New Guinea, Malaysia, and the Philippines, home to the most diverse coral reefs in the world, where coral reefs evolved hundreds of millions of years ago. It is unfortunately the place where reef bombing and cyanide fishing are practiced most.

Bearded scorpion fish hunting sweepers, Myanmar. Bearded scorpion fish are excellent camouflage artists. They often blend in perfectly with their surroundings, as this one has amongst soft coral. The scorpion fish, which got its name from its poisonous spine on its dorsal fin, will lie and wait until a sweeper comes close enough, then in a quick burst, swallow it whole.

Flamboyant cuttlefish are some of my favorite animals. They are small, growing to only 3 inches (8 cm) long, and instead of swimming like most cuttlefish, they walk along the sea floor, using their arms as modified feet. They wave their bright red arms around like samurai swords as they walk. When they find a small fish or invertebrate they're interested in eating, they change their color and texture to look just like their surroundings. Then they use one of their two tentacles to slowly reach out and grab their prey. Once they get their prey back into their arms, the flamboyant cuttlefish burst with colors, flashing red and yellow bands down their bodies.

Lake Kakaban, Indonesia is one of only two landlocked saltwater lakes in the world. The lake is surrounded by a huge ridge that has protected it from the outside world for thousands of years. The animals in the lake are unique, and live without large predators. Lake Kakaban is home to four species of jellyfish, and many fish and invertebrates that are only found in this lake.

FACING PAGE: **A Hawaiian turkeyfish, Oahu, Hawaii.** Turkeyfish are relatives of lionfish, and have poisonous spines on their fins. They can grow to the size of a basketball, and are voracious predators of small fish.

Australian Institute of Marine Sciences (AIMS) scientist, Katharina Fabricius studying the crown-of-thorns starfish, which is responsible for consuming vast amounts of coral of the Great Barrier Reef. The crown-of-thorns starfish is a natural species that usually grow and die out every 200 years. Run off from agriculture has reduced mortality in the larval stage of the crown-of-thorns, their cycles are now only five years, and the species is flourishing. They are a huge problem for tourism on the Barrier Reef, so scientists are scrambling to learn more about what can halt their population growth.

A triton shell hunting a crown-of-thorns starfish. Crown-of-thorns starfish have hard venomous spines, grow very rapidly, release millions of eggs and have few natural predators. If mutilated, each of their arms can grow into a new starfish. The triton shell feasts on crown-of-thorns, but tritons have been all but wiped out because their shells are prized curios.

Paul Watson aboard the *Ocean Warrior*. Paul was one of the original activists in Greenpeace, who has battled poachers for over 30 years, and has sunk a whole Norwegian whaling fleet. He started the Sea Shepherd Conservation Society in 1977 to enforce international law on the high seas.

SEA SHEPHERD

**"THERE IS NO SPECIES ON THIS PLANET THAT HAS EVER SURVIVED BY IGNORING THE BASIC LAWS OF ECOLOGY AND WE'RE NOW BREAKING THOSE BASIC LAWS EVERY DAY IN EVERY WAY AND THAT IS GOING TO BE OUR OWN DEMISE IN A VERY SHORT PERIOD OF TIME, UNLESS WE LEARN TO LIVE HARMONIOUSLY WITH OUR NATURAL WORLD."
—PAUL WATSON, FOUNDER, SEA SHEPHERD CONSERVATION SOCIETY**

I went to all the major conservation organizations and there was virtually no one doing anything to save sharks. Then I met up with Paul Watson, the renegade of the conservation movement and one of the original activists in Greenpeace. Watson started Sea Shepherd Conservation Society in 1977. Its mandate was to intervene directly to uphold international conservation laws, regulations and treaties. It is not just a protest organization; it fills a void to actually enforce international law on the high seas.

Paul was launching a campaign to stop shark poaching in the Galápagos and in Cocos, Costa Rica. Cocos is a tiny island in the middle of the Pacific, with the greatest concentration of sharks in the world. Like the Galápagos, Cocos is a national park and a World Heritage Site that lies around an extinct volcano in the middle of the Pacific that's teeming with life. A 12-mile (19-km) no-fishing zone is meant to be a sanctuary for sharks. Despite being protected on paper, Costa Rica lacks the political will to preserve wildlife in the area. Park rangers on the island are ill equipped, with only small dinghies to do battle with the many fishing boats that ply the island's waters. With little enforcement, fishermen raid the waters every day, decimating the shark populations.

The president of Costa Rica asked Paul Watson for Sea Shepherd's help to protect Cocos, and Watson asked me to join him.

There were few organizations working to protect sharks, so I jumped at the opportunity to join the expedition and quickly put together a small crew of three: myself; Douglas Braun, one of my best friends that I met while finishing university in Kenya, who was working as a biologist in Vancouver; and a third member, Geordie Gregg, a paramedic I'd taught scuba diving to a few years earlier. Doug, Geordie and I pulled together our 35 cases of HD video equipment and scuba gear and headed to Los Angeles to meet up with Watson.

We boarded the *Ocean Warrior*, Sea Shepherd's flagship, in Los Angeles and started our 14-day, 2,400-mile journey south to Costa Rica with a combined crew of 32 from all over North America. The ship is repainted and renamed on every new campaign to avoid being recognized by poachers and authorities. The *Ocean Warrior* has been in battles against poachers dozens of times, and proudly displays its

"kill flags" on the side of the ship—the flags of boats it has rammed or sunk. It is equipped with a "can opener"—a hydraulic steel blade that extends from the side of the ship in case of battle. The ship also has a "goo gun" that can fire pie filling hundreds of meters in addition to its water cannons, flare guns and butyric acid ("stink bombs"). This vessel is a warship unlike any other.

TOP: Kill flags adorn the side of the *Ocean Warrior*, representing the flags of boats Sea Shepherd has rammed or sunk.

LEFT: The crew of the *Ocean Warrior* pulling in illegally set longlines, and dealing with the huge amounts of monofilament line.

FACING PAGE: Sea Shepherd's flagship, the *Ocean Warrior*, is equipped with water cannons, a "can opener" (a hydraulic blade), a "goo gun," butyric acid ("stink bombs"), flare guns, and propeller fouling devices. It was our home for three very hot months during filming, most of which time we slept on the deck to avoid the heat in the cabins.

Sea Shepherd crew aboard an illegal fishing boat in the Galápagos. Sharks are of such high value that fishermen chance being arrested and having their ships confiscated to enter the Galápagos marine reserve to poach sharks.

FACING PAGE: **Paul Watson and the crew of the *Farley Mowat* (formerly the *Ocean Warrior*).** Sea Shepherd's flag is a modified Jolly Roger, or pirate flag, which is intimidating to poachers.

Isobel Alexander

Scott Quinn

Charles Hutchings

Dinah Y. Elissat

George (Geordie) M. Gregg

Captain Paul Watson

Allison Lance Watson

Nathan Meakes

Lilliolani (Lani) Lum-Watson

Douglas Braun

Joshua Trenter

S. Fraser Hall

EDWARD HALL

Tobago Watson

Ronald Colby

Nadia Winstead

Nathalie Le M

an (Norm) Waldhager

Linda Taylor

Kerrie Frason

Ryan Kurtz

Rob Stewart

Lisa Shalom

Patrick Sullivan

Susan ~~Gunther~~ Larsen

James (Jim) Gorman

Carlos Cembrero Perez

Rhian McKee

Stacie Nievaard

Madeline Ffitch

Pär Odin Löthman

Penelope (Penny) Carrangis

The crew of the Sea Shepherd's flagship, the *Ocean Warrior*, and the Sharkwater film crew of Douglas Braun, Geordie Gregg, and me.

Twelve days from Los Angeles, and 50 miles (80.5 km) inside Guatemalan waters, we found the *Varadero 1*, a long-lining fishing boat from Puntarenas, Costa Rica, illegally fishing for sharks. On instruction from authorities in Guatemala, Sea Shepherd ordered the *Varadero 1* to release any sharks that were caught, and to follow them to port in Guatemala.

THE BATTLE

"IMAGINE IF YOU WENT INTO THE FOREST AND YOU MADE SOME SORT OF TRAP LINE THAT CAUGHT MOOSE, DEER, SKUNKS, PORCUPINES, SQUIRRELS, DOGS. YOU KNOW, CAUGHT ALL THESE SPECIES, WHEN REALLY WHAT YOU WERE AFTER WERE ONE OR TWO BUT YOU HAD ALL THESE SPECIES THAT WERE CAUGHT, THAT WERE DYING OR DEAD. I MEAN CLEARLY IT WOULDN'T LAST A DAY. NOBODY COULD SET A TRAP LINE DOWN FOR 30 MILES AND THROW AWAY HALF THE ANIMALS HE OR SHE KILLED OR CAUGHT, NOBODY WOULD TOLERATE IT FOR A MINUTE, BUT IT'S GOING ON OUT THERE ON A MASSIVE SCALE EVERYDAY."
—MARK BUTLER, CONSERVATIONIST, ECOLOGY ACTION CENTER

Twelve days from Costa Rica, and 50 miles inside Guatemalan waters, we encountered the *Varadero 1*, a Costa Rican fishing boat with illegally set longlines. The *Varadero 1* was catching and killing sharks without a permit, and Guatemalan authorities requested that Sea Shepherd bring the rogue vessel in to port for arrest. In effect deputized by Guatemala to enforce its fishing laws, our new mission was to stop the *Varadero 1* from killing sharks, and bring its crew to justice.

Communicating by radio, we advised the fishermen to release the sharks on their lines. Despite our repeated warnings about their illegal actions, the crew continued to kill sharks, pulling them out of the sea, cutting off their fins in full view of our ship.

The sharks were incredibly important to the fishermen as they were well aware of the shark fins' value in Asia. Fins are so profitable that long-liners in decrepit boats around the world scour the oceans for sharks, even where it is illegal. Because keeping the unprofitable shark bodies requires expensive refrigeration systems, fishermen around the world started finning. Finning involves removing only the fins from sharks that are often still alive, and throwing the rest of the bodies overboard, wasting over 95 percent of the animal.

In an effort to stop the slaughter, Sea Shepherd's crew took direct action by attempting to take hold of the long lines before the *Varadero 1* could. Foiled in their efforts to take more sharks, the *Varadero 1* made a break for it after a tiring two-hour "tug-of-war" for the longlines. Realizing that their vessel would be confiscated by Guatemalan authorities if Sea Shepherd managed to seize the boat, the *Varadero 1* ran, with our ship in hot pursuit. In an effort to capture the poachers, Sea Shepherd fired water cannons at the vessel, trying to flood or stall the boat's engines.

After a tiring and heated six-hour battle, the two boats collided, with the *Varadero 1* finally surrendering and following us into port for arrest. Our victory was short-lived, however. A few hours from port, we received word by radio from Guatemalan authorities that a gunboat had been dispatched to arrest us! Someone, somewhere, was pulling strings and our situation was quickly getting complicated. We chose the best course of action we could under the circumstances. Instead of facing arrest and legal battles that we had little chance of winning, we abandoned the *Varadero 1* and headed south for Costa Rican waters.

The *Varadero 1*'s crew continued to land sharks despite being warned by Sea Shepherd that their activity was illegal, and that the Guatemalan government wanted them escorted in for arrest. Sea Shepherd ordered them to stop killing sharks, and they refused.

Finning sharks is illegal in Costa Rica, and the whole shark has to be brought into port intact to ensure the legality of the fishery. The crew of the *Varadero 1* continued dismembering sharks, throwing much of them overboard. This crew member threw the head of a silky shark towards us.

The Sea Shepherd crew trying to intervene and get to the long lines before the *Varadero 1*.

BOTTOM: Carlos, our translator, on the megaphone after receiving no response via radio.

The crew of the *Ocean Warrior* working to bring in the *Varadero 1*'s longlines, and release any sharks that were still alive. Dealing with miles of monofilament line and hooks by hand is very difficult work.

Once the illegally set longlines had been brought in, the *Varadero 1* fled to avoid being brought to Guatemala to face charges and possible confiscation of the ship. The *Ocean Warrior* pursued with water canons, in hopes of flooding or stalling their engines.

After hours of chasing the *Varadero 1*, the two ships collided. After the collision, the *Varadero 1* agreed to follow the *Ocean Warrior* into port for arrest. A few hours from port in Guatemala, we received word that a gun boat had been sent to arrest both the crew of the *Varadero 1* and us! The crew of the *Varadero 1* had obviously pulled some strings. Instead of facing arrest in Guatemala, Sea Shepherd decided to leave the *Varadero 1* and continue south to Costa Rica.

Shark fins were pushed off the roof of an illegal shark fin operation in Puntarenas to avoid being filmed by our cameras. In Puntarenas, on the coast of Costa Rica, there was a whole private bay full of shark fin operations. Fins are dried behind huge cement walls to prevent anyone from witnessing the activity. As soon as I started filming the fins drying on the roof, the employees stormed out of the building, trying to push the fins off the roof and out of sight of my camera. After switching locations, I took this shot of the fins on the ground.

COURT AND CORRUPT COSTA RICA

"SHARKS ARE DIFFICULT TO CONSERVE BECAUSE, ON ONE HAND, YOU HAVE PEOPLE AFRAID OF THEM AND NOT REALLY WANTING TO GO ANYWHERE NEAR THEM. PEOPLE CAN SORT OF FISH THEM WITH IMPUNITY, THERE IS NO ONE LOOKING AFTER THE SHARKS. THERE IS NO CAMPAIGN, LIKE A GREENPEACE CAMPAIGN TO SAVE THE SHARKS."
—PATRICK MOORE, GREENPEACE FOUNDER

On arrival in port, Costa Rican authorities boarded our boat. Our motley crew of environmentalists had made the top of the news after the crew of the *Varadero 1* claimed that we had tried to kill them. We discovered that we had been charged with seven counts of attempted murder for the seven crew members of the *Varadero 1*. Our crew of 32 people had multiple video cameras which captured the facts of our encounter with the *Varadero 1*, and the tapes revealed the truth of what transpired off the coast of Guatemala—that Sea Shepherd's crew had not tried to kill anyone. After we showed the prosecutor the footage, the case was dismissed. But then two more prosecutors were brought on, and the copies of the video footage were mysteriously "lost." The new prosecutors had the *Ocean Warrior* searched for the tapes, which I had already shipped home to safety in case we needed them as further evidence in our defense.

All of the press surrounding our case brought us into contact with a conservationist named William who believed there was a connection between the Taiwanese mafia and our arrest. He explained that the shark fishing industry in Costa Rica was largely run by the Taiwanese. Shark finning is illegal in Costa Rica, but Costa Rican fins were turning up all over Asia, and there were rumors about huge Taiwanese fishing operations dedicated to processing shark fins. William brought us to a private bay where a myriad of Taiwanese shark fishing operations were at work. Costa Rican fishermen must land their catch at public docks that are checked for fins, but the illegal finners escape scrutiny by landing at the private coves. Finning operations that William showed us were hidden behind huge concrete walls to prevent prying eyes from witnessing what was happening.

We found a trailer next to one of these operations, and climbed on top to get a better vantage point from which to film. What we discovered and filmed were tens of thousands of fins drying on the rooftop of the building behind the wall. The employees in the finning plant soon noticed our presence and clambered onto the roof desperately trying to push the fins out of sight. They then stormed towards us, at which time we retreated to our "getaway" car and sped off with our valuable footage in hand.

Arriving back on the ship after our brush with the Taiwanese, we heard from our lawyer that the coast guard was on its way to arrest us. Instead of facing prison in Costa Rica, where you can be detained

The day after we arrived in Costa Rica, we were charged with seven counts of attempted murder. The coast guard ship brought police, detectives, lawyers and judges aboard the *Ocean Warrior* to investigate, and to search for my tapes of the incident. Luckily, I'd shipped the tapes home the night before. We were placed under house arrest on the ship in Puntarenas harbor.

Paul in the Puntarenas courthouse with Carlos, our translator, and Milton, our lawyer. It made no sense why we were being investigated and the *Varadero 1* was set free. We were invited by the president of Costa Rica to protect against shark poaching, and the *Varadero 1* was poaching sharks. We knew there was some deeper meaning to all this.

indefinitely until charges against you are investigated, Paul decided to make a break for international waters.

Guarded by coast guard ships, we pulled anchor, and ran barbed wire around the *Ocean Warrior*'s gunwales to prevent the coast guard from jumping onboard. Within minutes, the coast guard was right next to us waving machine guns to force us to stop. Our translator Carlos kept telling us, "They're going to shoot! They're going to shoot!" With luck, we made it out of Costa Rican waters without harm and the coast guard vessel gave up its pursuit and turned back. We continued southwest to the Galápagos, leaving Cocos to the poachers. The fins were worth too much money and there was a whole industry behind it. We knew we could never go back to Costa Rica.

Paul and me with Carlos on deck of the *Ocean Warrior*, while running from Costa Rica and being chased by the Coast Guard, who claimed they would shoot if we didn't stop.

After exposing corruption between the Costa Rican government and the Taiwanese shark finning operations, the authorities wanted to detain Paul Watson indefinitely, under charge of seven counts of attempted murder. Instead of going to prison, we made a break for international waters with the machine-gun-waving Costa Rican coast guard in hot pursuit.

Shark fins drying on the roof of an illegal shark fin operation in Puntarenas, Costa Rica. There was a whole bay of illegal shark fin operations that the authorities were ignoring. These operations were run by the Taiwanese mafia, and had private unregulated docks, guarded by huge cement walls. Taiwan was also a huge investor in Costa Rica, building major highways, bridges and buildings.

I climbed onto the roof of a trailer to film over the huge cement walls hiding the fin operation. As soon as they saw me, employees ran out onto the roof and tried pushing the fins off the roof, and out of sight of my camera. They then ran at us, forcing us to flee. Back at the ship, our lawyer called, saying that the police were on their way to detain Paul indefinitely. Paul decided we had to run for international waters, so we wrapped the *Ocean Warrior* with barbed wire to prevent the coast guard from jumping onboard and made a break for it. The coast guard chased us waving machine guns, saying they would shoot if we don't stop.

Galápagos giant tortoise, Santa Cruz Island, Galápagos Islands, Ecuador. Giant tortoises can grow to 550 pounds (250 kg) and live for more than 150 years.

HEADING TO THE GALÁPAGOS

"WE KNOW THAT PREDATORS ARE FUNDAMENTALLY CONTROLLING THE STRUCTURE AND FUNCTIONING OF THE ECOSYSTEMS. SHARKS ARE PROBABLY THE MOST THREATENED GROUP OF SPECIES THAT WE HAVE IN THE OCEAN RIGHT NOW. YOU'RE REMOVING A REALLY IMPORTANT CONTROLLING AGENT AND THAT COULD CAUSE UPHEAVAL IN THE LOWER TROPIC LEVELS LIKE THE PLANTS AND THE ZOOPLANKTON. THIS IS NOT A NATURAL PHENOMENON. IT'S BECAUSE OF FISHING AND OTHER HUMAN IMPACTS AND THERE IS A LOT WE CAN DO ABOUT THIS TO CHANGE IT." —DR. BORIS WORM, BIOLOGIST, DALHOUSIE UNIVERSITY

Paul Watson and Sea Shepherd had been invited to the Galápagos Islands by the Galápagos National Park, the agency responsible for maintaining and protecting the islands and their resources. Two years earlier, Sea Shepherd had donated a ship called the *Sirenian* to the national park to aid park officers in apprehending poachers. Without Sea Shepherd crew aboard to patrol the national park, and with many of the poachers being friends and relatives of Galápagos park officers, the *Sirenian* was ineffective at stemming the poaching.

Though the Galápagos National Park wanted Sea Shepherd there, the Ecuadorian Navy actually had authority over the park, as well as control over who could enter it. One year earlier, Sea Shepherd exposed a corruption ring within the Ecuadorian Navy, resulting in the second in command and many others losing their jobs. Due to the embarrassment brought about by Sea Shepherd in the past, the navy denied Sea Shepherd entry to the Galápagos. With the *Ocean Warrior* in need of repair, however, a temporary stay was granted by the navy and the ship was allowed to dock for 15 days.

I developed a pain in my left hip, which put a damper on the trip while I went to the hospital to have it checked out. The medical personnel said it was nothing, but two days later, the pain had increased, and I returned to the hospital. I was sent away this time with pain killers and anti-inflammatories. Two days later, the pain had increased so I returned to the hospital again, and tests were done. The results couldn't have been worse: a staphylococcus infection (often referred to as flesh-eating disease) had taken hold and a red line, revealing the advance of the infection, was working its way up my thigh. The infection had likely come from tiny cuts on my feet, and it had infected my lymphatic system—the reason for the pain in my hip.

Our translator managed to explain the situation, while several Spanish-speaking doctors and nurses spoke about the situation in front of me. Their sawing gestures were unnerving, to say the least, as one of the most common remedies for a staph infection is to remove the infected tissue and the limb. Geordie Gregg, our assistant and paramedic, had tragic stories of friends who had similar, but less serious, infections that resulted in the amputation of their legs. The gravity of the situation was serious and I was faced with a big decision: try out the local medical system or beeline it back to North America for medical attention closer to home.

Waves wash against the rocky shores of San Cristobal Island, Galápagos Islands, Ecuador. The marine reserve was created in 1998, and at the time, it was one of the largest marine reserves in the world. The waters surrounding the Galápagos Islands are home to 3,000 species of marine plants and animals.

A Galápagos giant tortoise. Giant tortoises have two different types of shells. One has a huge saddle shaped arc allowing their necks to stretch up so they can feed from higher shrubs and branches. The other shell design lacks the saddle, and the tortoises feed mostly on or near the ground.

A marine iguana and a lava lizard sunning themselves, Floreana Island, Galápagos Islands, Ecuador. Marine iguanas are vegetarians, but lava lizards, named as they are often the color of lava rocks, feed on insects. They are both endemic to the Galápagos.

Courting waved albatrosses, Espanola Island, Galápagos Islands, Ecuador. These are huge birds with 11-foot (3.35-m) wing spans. Waved albatrosses live most of their lives on the open ocean, only finding their way to land once a year to mate, lay eggs, and rear their chicks. Albatross populations around the world are suffering greatly, as they are often caught as by-catch in longline fisheries.

The sound stage at Technicolor in Toronto, with our sound mixer, Steve Foster. Mixing the sound for *Sharkwater* was a phenomenal experience. Every day we concentrated on how much and which of the hundreds of sounds we wanted to hear from each speaker.

END OF THE ODYSSEY

"UNLESS PEOPLE ARE PREPARED TO DEVOTE THEIR LIVES TO SOLVING THESE PROBLEMS, NOTHING IS REALLY GOING TO CHANGE. BUT YOU DON'T NEED EVERYBODY. YOU JUST SIMPLY NEED A SMALL PERCENTAGE. FIVE TO SEVEN PERCENT IS STARTING TO MAKE A BIG IMPACT." —PAUL WATSON, FOUNDER OF SEA SHEPHERD CONSERVATION SOCIETY

After leaving the hospital, I decided we needed to get footage at Cocos Island. We had filmed in Galápagos, but to complete the story of sharks in the area, we needed to film at Cocos. We snuck back into Costa Rica using public transportation and school buses to avoid being detected. Instead of Costa Rica being lost to the poachers, our trials in Costa Rica had helped shed light on the illegal shark fishing operations. People were furious and they began to rally in the streets against the private docks. Our efforts hadn't been a total failure.

We continued on to Cocos to film hammerheads in all their glory, while Costa Ricans, led by a conservation group called Pretoma, fought the government to stop the finning.

Upon returning home from four months in Costa Rica and Ecuador, I was faced with the monumental task of becoming a filmmaker. I had to figure out what to do with the 100 some odd hours of footage from the trip. I also had to piece together and edit a human drama (when I expected to have a shark documentary) and make it compelling enough to change people's perception of sharks. I was also exhausted, and a little sick from all of the events of the last four months.

Back in Canada, there were technical challenges to even watching all of the high-definition (HD) footage I'd acquired. HD decks were prohibitively expensive to rent, and I had 137 tapes to go through, and a movie to create. I edited together a three-minute trailer for the film, and planned to pitch the film at festivals and to broadcasters around the world.

During the first film event I attended in Santa Barbara, California, I started feeling quite ill. My muscles felt as though they were working differently and my skin was hypersensitive. Doctors prescribed flu remedies, and I returned to Toronto. The strange illness prevailed, and I saw specialist after specialist. Doctors thought I had mono, depression or chronic fatigue syndrome. After months of illness, fatigue, shakes and the inability to sleep, I finally got an appointment with the head of tropical medicine in Canada. He conducted numerous tests, and told me that I had dengue fever, West Nile virus and tuberculosis. I was put on antibiotics for eight months for tuberculosis, and was told that my body was fighting off the other two viruses.

I continued to attend film festivals at reduced capacity—trying to get broadcasters and distributors excited about the film. Everyone saw great potential, but they were skeptical of my ability as a first time

David Hannan using the HD edit bay at Pro-Cam in Brisbane, Australia. We filmed in Australia and the surrounding areas for more than a year, and spent weekends pulling all nighters, logging and making selects from the hundreds of hours of HD material we'd shot.

director. Ultimately, I could choose to partner with another production company, or find another way to get the film off the ground.

The shark footage I shot did garner some interest though, particularly from a famous Australian cinematographer named David Hannan. Hannan had a project to shoot on the Great Barrier Reef, and invited me to shoot with him in Australia. Our deal was unique, allowing me to keep the footage that I shot for my own use. Filming underwater was my favorite thing to do, and after nine months of illness and big-city living, tropical Australia sounded perfect. The invitation would also give me the ability to continue working on *Sharkwater*.

I moved to Australia, spending over a year shooting on the Great Barrier Reef, throughout Southeast Asia and the South Pacific. We continued filming *Sharkwater* over four-and-a-half years in a total of 15 countries. What started in Central and South America became a journey that changed my life forever.

Finally, all the effort I had put in and the time to think about the project gave me the confidence to start putting *Sharkwater* together.

I returned to Toronto where friend and expert editor Michael Clark had just finished his latest project. It was the perfect opportunity to work together and to finish a feature documentary about man's relationship with sharks and the exploitation of the oceans. Michael and I worked around the clock for two years, cutting down 400 hours of material into 90 minutes. We pulled the story together, and with the help of a few more expert editors (Rik Morden, Tippy Bushkin and Jeremy Stuart), we finished the film, and the rest is history.

Nate Scripture and me filming on North Stradbroke Island, Queensland, Australia, where we lived for much of our time.

The *Sharkwater* crew (from left: Mike Schram, Tyler MacLeod, Rob Stewart, Christopher Chin, and below, Erica Cox) diving in Curaçao, during the Curaçao Dive Festival where *Sharkwater* screened on the beach in June 2007.

**Filming Caribbean reef sharks in
the Bahamas for a shoot with
*Entertainment Tonight Canada.***
I taught host Rick Campanelli from *ET* how
to dive and brought him diving with sharks
for a TV piece on the film.
PHOTO: STUART COVE'S

Me filming a humpback whale in Tonga. Despite being enormous in size, humpbacks are incredibly aware of their surroundings, and what their enormous flukes are doing. The flukes would often fly by within inches of me, as the humpback frolicked for the camera. This humpback was a teenage female that particularly liked people, even though she had scars on her body from nets and fishing gear.

Self-portrait, Cod Hole, Great Barrier Reef, Australia. When I started out as an underwater photographer, I was 18. When magazines wanted pictures of me for their articles or contributor sections, I was worried they wouldn't take me seriously because of my age, so I sent them underwater shots!

FACING PAGE: **Filming underwater with Feather, the largest of the three underwater camera housings we filmed with.** Feather was built by David Hannan in Australia to house Sony HDCam cameras and LCD monitors. Feather weighs 80 kilograms, and is so huge that a crane is needed to get the camera in and out of the water. The size is advantageous underwater, making camera movements very smooth.

David Hannan filming with Feather (a camera system) in the Coral Sea, Australia. The Coral Sea was an absolute pleasure to film in. Compared to the Galápagos' cold water and currents, the warm, clear water of the Coral Sea was perfect for filming colorful reef creatures, and easy diving from the back of the boat.

Niphon, a coral reef scientist from Thailand, preparing for a dive, Similan Islands, Thailand. The Similan Islands were incredible, full of beautiful soft coral and thriving reef systems.

The view from the top of Bartolome Island, Galápagos Islands, Ecuador.
The Galápagos are a new archipelago—the youngest islands are still forming, due to a 2005 volcanic eruption. Much of the life in the Galápagos arrived via wind or ocean currents from South and Central America. Being isolated for so long has allowed species to change and adapt to the rugged and dry islands, creating many endemic species, found nowhere else on earth.

A sunset from the North Shore, Hawaii. The Hawaiian Islands are another Pacific archipelago born by volcanic eruption, though much older than the Galápagos. Evidence of the Hawaiian Islands' origins is still present on the Big Island, where lava flows into the sea, increasing the size of the island each year.

PREVIOUS PAGES: **Freediving in the Similan Islands, Thailand.** Freediving is a great way to get close to fast-moving animals such as dolphins and whales.

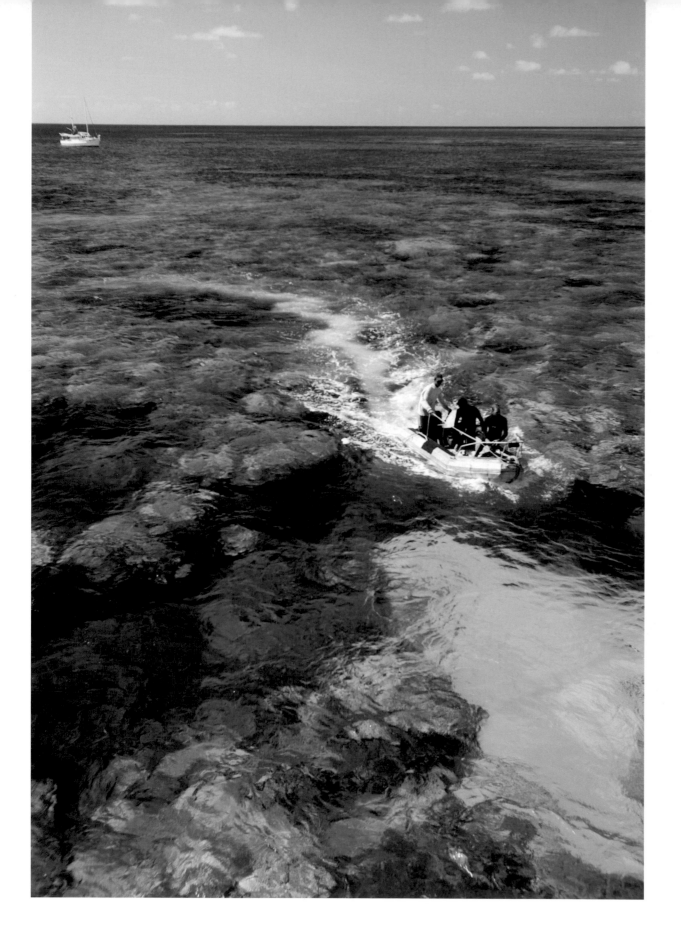

The *Foundation 1* crew scouting reefs, Great Barrier Reef, Australia. The Foundation One is an Australian Fisheries ship dedicated to crown-of-thorns eradication. The crew patrols the Great Barrier Reef, trying to save the coral with acid injection guns to kill crown-of-thorns starfish one arm at a time.

Lankayan Island, Sabah, Malaysian Borneo. Sabah has some of the best diving in the world. Beautiful diverse reefs, bizarre creatures and incredibly friendly people make Sabah one of my favorite places to dive.

Caribbean reef sharks vying for food thrown from Stuart Cove's boat, Nassau Bahamas. There are many misconceptions about sharks: that they attack at the first sign of blood; that they go into a frenzy, attacking anything in sight; that they're primitive eating machines or predators of people. Untrue. Sharks are highly evolved and sophisticated animals that make mistakes once in a while, and bite a human. Even when a shark does make a mistake, flesh is rarely removed, as the shark realizes it bit something it didn't want, and lets go. More people are killed by lightning than by sharks!

The media makes money portraying sharks as dangerous monsters. Reversing the media's portrayal, and the impression of films such as *Jaws* is difficult, as very few people actually get to encounter a shark to change their opinion. Even the word "shark" comes from the Anglo-Saxon words "cut" and "villain." Finding a new view of sharks is essential to the public fighting for their protection. Elephants kill 100 people a year, yet an elephant dies and the world is up in arms. Sharks kill five people a year. We kill 100 million sharks every year, and their populations have declined by an estimated 90 percent in 30 years.

A diver with a bull ray, *Yongala* wreck, Queensland, Australia.
The loss of sharks around the world has caused their prey—smaller sharks, skates and rays—to explode in numbers. These rays have decimated shellfish fisheries off the east coast of North America. Due to the decline in scallops, many commercially sold scallops are now actually disks of flesh cut from rays.

Whitetip reef sharks hunting at night, while a parrot fish hides amongst the coral, Cocos Island, Costa Rica. Parrot fish secrete a mucous cocoon around them while they sleep. Breaking the mucous layer wakes the fish up to give it extra time to escape.

Silvertip shark, Coral Sea, Australia. This silvertip shark became disoriented in my lights, and ran right into my lens!

Hordes of whitetip reef sharks hunting in my lights at night, Cocos Island, Costa Rica. I spent hours every night following these sharks around while they hunted. White tip reef sharks use ampullae of Lorenzini on their snouts to detect fish hiding amongst coral at night. When one senses a fish, dozens of sharks go for it, forcing themselves into crevices in the reef to try and get at the hiding fish

FACING PAGE: **Whitetip reef shark chasing a squirrelfish at night, Cocos Island, Costa Rica.**

Yellowfin tuna at Cocos Island, Costa Rica. Leaps in fishing technology—including sonar and helicopters—have made fishing for tuna far too efficient. Yellowfin tuna are prized for sushi, and are worth an enormous amount of money. Their populations have dropped more than 90 percent.

Great white shark, South Africa.

Great white sharks are the most feared of all sharks. They can grow to 23 feet long (7 m) and 5,000 pounds (2300 kg), and we are just beginning to learn more about them, including that they will migrate thousands of miles. They're actually very difficult to get close to without using chum or blood in the water to attract them. Most great white shark attacks are actually investigatory bites or mistakes, and the shark rarely returns for another bite, or consumes any flesh. This clearly shows there is no intent by the shark to eat the human.

PHOTO: STUART WESTMORLAND

Whale shark, Cocos Island, Costa Rica. Whale sharks are the world's largest fish. They can reach 50 feet long and weigh 16 tons. They are gentle giants that feed by filtering tiny plankton from the water using their enormous mouths. Whale sharks are world travelers, often showing up in the same place year after year to feed on plankton blooms or coral spawns.

Two crocodile fish hide in the sand, waiting for unsuspecting prey to stumble upon them. Bottom trawlers drag huge weighted nets along the sea floor, scooping up everything in their paths, including many non-commercial fish, like crocodile fish as by-catch. Fish have air bladders, which are tiny air-filled sacks in their bodies that control their buoyancy. When they're pulled to the surface of the water in nets, the pressure of the water is removed, their swim bladders explode, and the fish die. An estimated 54 billion pounds of fish are wasted this way every year, while eight million people die of starvation.

A soapfish hiding amongst orange cup corals and feather dusters at Town Pier, Bonaire. Town Pier is a shipping pier that is home to an enormous amount of underwater life. Much of the life comes out to hunt at night, the best time to dive there.

A sargassum frogfish hangs out in flotsam or patches of seaweed that float around the open ocean, Mantanani Island, Malaysian Borneo.
Much of the open ocean is desert, so any animals in the open sea like to hang around structures where there is shelter. Sargassum frogfish hang out in the seaweed, gobbling up tiny fish and invertebrates.

A Commerson's frogfish yawning, Kapalai Island, Malaysian Borneo. Frogfish have enormous mouths, capable of swallowing fish nearly as large as they are. They're ambush predators that look just like their surroundings, waiting for unsuspecting victims to wander by. Their huge mouths open so rapidly that a vacuum is created, and the fish are literally sucked into their mouths.

A painted frogfish, Lankayan Island, Malaysian Borneo.
Frogfish come in all shapes and sizes, from basketball-sized to the golf ball–sized painted frogfish, named for a spot on their sides.

Ornate ghost pipefish, Kapalai Island, Sabah, Malaysian Borneo. Ghost pipefish are relatives of the seahorse. The males carry their eggs in huge pouches on their stomachs. They spend their days hiding amongst algae and coral trying to avoid being seen by predators. They have no natural defenses except camouflage.

Mating mandarin fish, Kapalai Island, Malaysian Borneo. Their ritual lasts only seconds at sunset while they both leave the safety of the reef to swim out into open water, releasing sperm and eggs simultaneously.

Mating green sea turtles, Sipadan Island, Malaysian Borneo. Every species of sea turtle is endangered due to being harvested for their meat and shells. Many of their nesting beaches have also been developed. Their eggs are also prized throughout much of Asia, and are harvested within hours of being laid.

Spotted coral trout, Great Barrier Reef, Australia.

Decorator crab with a sponge attached to its back, Town Pier, Bonaire. These crabs attach anything they can find to their backs to disguise and camouflage themselves.

A school of jacks swim by a soft coral colony, Sipadan Islands, Thailand. Soft coral is an animal, not a plant. They filter plankton and organic matter out of the water during currents, swelling up to take in more water and filter out more food. This same soft coral colony was one half the size, looking like a wilted flower only 30 minutes later.

Schooling anthias on the Great Barrier Reef, Australia. The Great Barrier Reef is the largest living organism in the world, covering 230,000 square miles (370,000 square kilometers), and is the only one visible from outer space. It is a huge tourist attraction, bringing in more than a billion dollars a year. Twenty-eight million tons of sediment flow from agricultural run off onto the reef each year, killing the coral, and bringing nutrients into the water, allowing the crown-of-thorns starfish to flourish and eat the coral.

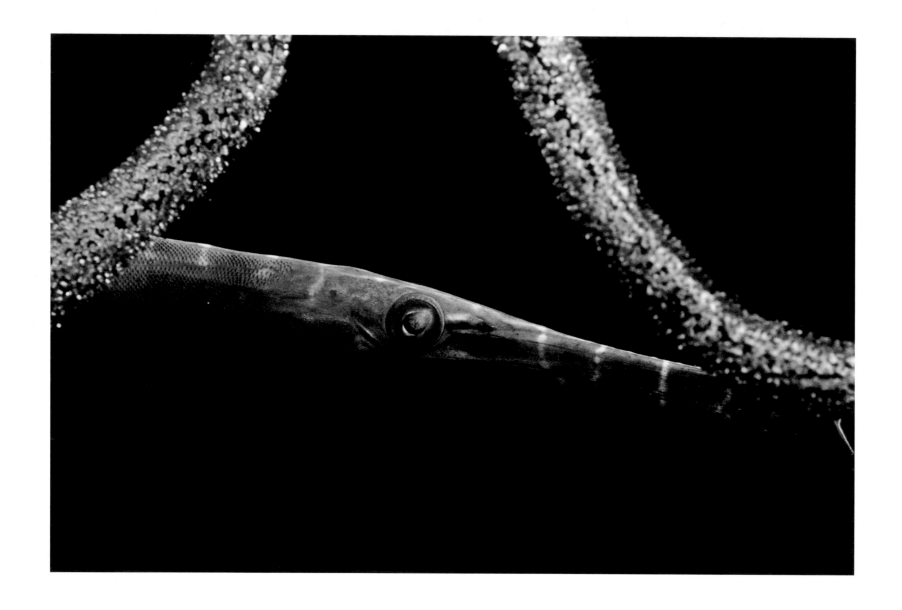

A trumpetfish eye, hiding behind a whip coral, Bonaire. Trumpetfish are interesting animals, and a joy to watch. Sometimes they hide amongst other long, thin structures, like coral or weeds. Other times they like to hang out with other fish, flanking a jack's every move. Trumpetfish use their long mouths to suck in small fish and invertebrates.

Two bicolor blennies hiding in coral, Myanmar. In the ocean, there is life in virtually every crevice. These blennies warily hide in the coral, snapping up morsels of food when they float by. They can also be quite territorial, fighting other blennies for prime real estate.

A manta ray and a mobula ray swimming together, Cocos Island, Costa Rica. Mantas and mobulas are known as "devil rays" of which there are nine different species. The manta is the largest, and is distinguished from the others because their mouths are at the very front of their bodies, where in mobulas, the mouth is underneath their head.

Schooling scalloped hammerhead sharks, Cocos Island, Costa Rica. Scalloped hammerheads can grow to 14 feet long, and eat fish, invertebrates and stingrays. They are often found with stingray barbs in their face. Scalloped hammerheads are especially vulnerable to overfishing due to their tendency to come together in groups, and to frequent seamounts.

Dusky shark attacking a ball of sardines, South Africa. Sharks move in a four-dimensional world, making it much more difficult for them to catch prey than a fox chasing a rabbit on the ground. Sharks often try to eliminate pathways of escape and make feeding easier by schooling the fish into a ball at the surface. These "bait balls" also attract other predators in the area, including dolphins, whales, tuna, billfish, seabirds and sea lions. PHOTO: PETER LAMBERTI

Caribbean reef shark face, Bahamas. Meeting eyes with a shark for the first time is a profound experience that can change someone's impression of sharks dramatically.

Feeding a Caribbean reef shark, Bahamas. Shark-diving tourism is a booming industry, flourishing in the Caribbean, South Africa, Australia and Polynesia among other places. Most people afraid of sharks have never been in the water with one, making shark tourism important for changing public perception of these misunderstood creatures. The tourism industry can also save shark populations when the sharks are worth more alive in tourism dollars than they are dead for their fins.

A scalloped hammerhead shark aggressive display, Wolf Island, Galápagos Islands, Ecuador. Aggressive displays amongst females in a school tell subordinate females to move away from the desired center of the school. The dominant females will arch their backs, sway their heads from side to side, spin, and thrash about to show the smaller females who's boss. The center of the school is where males are thought to enter the school to find their mates.

Me freediving in the Bahamas with Caribbean reef sharks. It was important for us to show a different relationship with sharks that people hadn't seen before. Freediving with sharks is one of my favorite past times, and it helps demonstrate that they are not predators of people.

181

Holding a Caribbean reef shark, Bahamas. More public awareness and pressure to protect sharks will fuel more legislation, research and exposure. Wide-scale shark fishing really only began in the late 1980s when China began trading with the rest of the world, and its economy boomed, making shark fin soup accessible to hundreds of millions more people. For shark populations to survive, there needs to be a global ban on shark finning, and a shark fishing commission set up to regulate those fisheries that are sustainable.

Me with a potato cod, Cod Hole, Great Barrier Reef, Australia. Giant potato cod are a favorite of divers on the Barrier Reef, where numerous tour operators feed them for tourists.

Caribbean reef sharks, Bahamas. This reef shark has a remora attached to it. Remoras have disks on their heads that allow them to attach to larger animals. They detach to scoop up scraps when the sharks feed, and reattach for travel.

Milton, our 15-foot fiberglass shark mascot named after our Costa Rican lawyer, Milton, posing at a mall in Ft. Lauderdale, Florida.

THE LAUNCH

"FUTURE GENERATIONS ARE GOING TO LOOK BACK ON US AND THEY ARE GOING TO THINK OF US AS BARBARIANS, THE SAME WAY WE THINK OF THE SLAVE TRADERS. THEY'RE GOING TO LOOK AT US AS BARBARIANS FOR WHAT WE ARE DOING, THE FACT THAT WE'RE BURNING ALL THE FOSSIL FUELS IN A FEW GENERATIONS, THAT WE WIPED OUT THE OCEANS, THAT WE'VE DRIVEN SPECIES TO EXTINCTION, AND WORSE, THIS IS THE WORST PART, WE KNOW WHAT WE ARE DOING. THE SCIENTISTS KNOW, THE ENVIRONMENTALISTS KNOW, THE COMPANIES KNOW, AND THE GENERAL PUBLIC KNOWS, AND YET WE ARE ALLOWING OURSELVES TO DO IT." —REX WYLER, FOUNDER GREENPEACE INTERNATIONAL, AUTHOR

After editing for two years, and shooting additional footage in numerous countries, we finally completed *Sharkwater*. Our team of editors, assistant editors, composers, sound designers, sound editors and marketing gurus worked day and night to launch the film at the Toronto International Film Festival in 2006. We had two film screenings during the festival—the first for an audience of 1,000. The creation of the film often felt like betting double or nothing. We invested more and more into the film in the belief that it would fly, but never really knowing for sure.

We received standing ovations at both screenings, and we all sighed with happiness and relief when the film received this seal of approval from the audiences.

We went on to present *Sharkwater* at some of the most prestigious festivals in the world. From Toronto, we continued on to the Atlantic Film Festival. I was exhausted and sick by this point, so I spent the entire time in bed, except for a 30-minute question-and-answer session after the screening. We won the People's Choice Award. We then flew to Hawaii for the Hawaii International Film Festival, where we screened the film on Waikiki beach for 8,000 people, and won the Jury Award. At the same time, *Sharkwater* was playing in France at the World Festival of Underwater Pictures, where it won two more awards. At the Fort Lauderdale International Film Festival, along with my old friend David Garland, *Sharkwater* won the People's Choice, the Best Documentary, and the Spirit of Independents awards.

Sharkwater hit theaters in Canada as a test market on March 23, 2007, breaking opening weekend box-office records for a documentary.

TO DATE, *SHARKWATER* HAS WON 17 AWARDS

CANADA'S TOP TEN—TORONTO INTERNATIONAL FILM FESTIVAL

PEOPLE'S CHOICE—ATLANTIC FILM FESTIVAL

PEOPLE'S CHOICE—FORT LAUDERDALE INTERNATIONAL FILM FESTIVAL

BEST DOCUMENTARY—FORT LAUDERDALE INTERNATIONAL FILM FESTIVAL

SPIRIT OF INDEPENDENTS AWARD—FORT LAUDERDALE INTERNATIONAL FILM FESTIVAL

SPECIAL JURY AWARD—HAWAII INTERNATIONAL FILM FESTIVAL

BEST MUSICAL COMPOSITION—FRANCE WORLD FESTIVAL OF UNDERWATER PICTURES

PRIX PLANETE THALASSA—FRANCE WORLD FESTIVAL OF UNDERWATER PICTURES

BEST OF THE FESTIVAL—PALM SPRINGS INTERNATIONAL FILM FESTIVAL

BEST INTERNATIONAL DOC—BEVERLY HILLS HI-DEF FESTIVAL

BEST HD FEATURE—AFI DALLAS INTERNATIONAL FILM FESTIVAL

AUDIENCE CHOICE AWARD FOR BEST FEATURE—GEN ART FILM FESTIVAL

GRAND JURY AWARD FOR BEST FEATURE—GEN ART FILM FESTIVAL

PETER BENCHLEY SHARK CONSERVATION AWARD—SHARK RESEARCH INSTITUTE

THE MUST-SEE AWARD—TELLURIDE MOUNTAINFILM FESTIVAL

HERO OF CONSERVATION AWARD—CONSERVATION FOR THE OCEANS FOUNDATION

I was honored by the Honolulu City Council for my work creating *Sharkwater*. The certificate was presented by Donovan Dela Cruz (holding the certificate), a long-time friend, and great conservationist.

Milton pictured at the International Fishing Hall of Fame in Ft. Lauderdale, Florida. Fishermen and hunters are often some of the most outspoken conservationists, and are often the first to notice when a species has been exploited. It's important to engage all audiences with the message of preserving the oceans to sustain human life on earth.

At the International Fishing Hall of Fame, I spoke to a large group of boy scouts about sharks, their importance, and how easy it is for kids to get involved and make a difference.

At the Hawaii International Film Festival, *Sharkwater* screened on Waikiki beach for 8,000 people. This was a highlight of our film festival tour, as Hawaiian culture and mythology deeply respects sharks.

Signing autographs at the Jules Verne Film Festival in Paris, France. When I set out to make *Sharkwater* it was supposed to be a pretty underwater film. We started filming ourselves to keep ourselves out of prison in Costa Rica, and four years later I'm signing autographs, which was totally unexpected.

Lā'au Melomelo (Bait/Chum stick)
Made from Kauila (A Native Tree)

Makau Manō
Shark Hook

My hand in front of a traditional
Polynesian shark hook on
display in Hawaii.

THREATS FACING SHARKS

- **OVER 100 MILLION SHARKS ARE KILLED ANNUALLY**
- **SHARKS KILL ABOUT 5 PEOPLE EACH YEAR**
- **ELEPHANTS AND TIGERS KILL 100 PEOPLE ANNUALLY**
- **ILLEGAL DRUGS KILL 22,000 PEOPLE ANNUALLY**
- **STARVATION KILLS 8,000,000 ANNUALLY**

Shark populations around the world are estimated to have declined by 90 percent, with most recent studies from Dalhousie University showing declines ranging from 93 to 99 percent in the Atlantic Ocean. Julia Baum, Ransom Myers and other scientists at Dalhousie University studying shark populations have, for the first time, shown the dire consequences of declining shark populations. When sharks as apex predators are removed from the top of the food chain, their natural prey, smaller skates and rays explode in numbers. In turn, these smaller predators decimate shellfish populations, wiping out century-old shellfish fisheries, and the livelihoods of many people who depend on the ocean to provide for their families.

Without a doubt, removing sharks from the oceans will have serious consequences. In fact, the eradication of predators from ecosystems has traditionally been far more devastating than could be predicted.

Take the case of the innocent sea otter, which, as a species, is less than 8 million years old. Sought after for their pelts, sea otters were all but wiped out on the west coast of North America. The sea urchin population, which the otters fed on, exploded. With the urchin population left unchecked, they ravaged vast amounts of kelp, destroying the underwater kelp forests and robbing the herring of its breeding ground. Without the herring populations to feed on, much of the ecosystem suffered.

The situation with sharks is very similar, except man is removing a predator that's been shaping the ecosystems in every ocean for over 400 million years, and the ecosystems that will be affected include our own.

We depend on the oceans for survival, not just to feed much of the planet, but also for 70 percent of the oxygen we breathe. Phytoplankton in the oceans that sits below sharks in the food web consumes more carbon dioxide (CO_2)—the global warming gas—than anything else on earth.

Without healthy oceans, we affect the quality of the air we breathe and all life in the environment. Wiping out the oceans' largest, most long-lasting predator before we fully understand the ecology of the oceans will undoubtedly have disastrous consequences, especially in a world afflicted by global warming.

Currently, given our present consumption patterns, we will need six planet earths to sustain life based on the resources we use in the western world. All fisheries worldwide are estimated to collapse by 2048. While

Many sharks I encounter in the wild have hooks in their mouths, evidence of enormous fishing pressure. These are the lucky survivors.

eight million people die of starvation each year, we waste an estimated 54 billion pounds of fish meat annually as by-catch.

Our relationship with the natural world is clearly not working, and it's not sharks or the environment that's at stake, it's us. We're causing the extinction of more species within our lifetime than have gone extinct in the last 65 million years. Sharks survived five major extinctions, and they will survive this one. The question is, how many of our future generations will go lacking, suffer starvation and crisis because we've failed to recognize that we are living in an unsustainable way?

Also consider that we currently dump six million tons of pollutants into the oceans each year. Many of these pollutants, including heavy metals such as mercury, accumulate in living matter. Predators consuming smaller creatures accumulate the pollutants from their food, becoming extremely toxic themselves. Orcas and beluga whales washing up on shores in the St. Lawrence are now treated as hazardous waste. Large predators like sharks, tunas, billfish, salmon and others also accumulate toxins in staggering quantities. Not only is it advisable not to eat them because they're almost gone, but they're also toxic.

Threats facing the ocean are numerous. We're destroying ecosystems necessary for survival. Mangrove swamps, which are nurseries to baby fish, are being developed and polluted. Fishing methods such as bottom trawling drag huge weighted nets along the sea floor, scooping up all animals and the ecosystem in their paths. Many fisheries are also incredibly wasteful. Some, like the bottom trawlers, or shrimp fisheries, waste 85 percent of what they bring to the surface as by-catch.

Shark-targeted longlines are very much the same. They catch birds, turtles, sea lions, rays and myriad fish, when only a few species are actually desired. Today, an estimated 70 million of the 100 million sharks killed each year are caught for fins. The Asian demand for shark fin soup has soared since the late 1980s when China began trade with the rest of the world. A single pound of fin now fetches over $300. Not bad, considering the fin is tasteless, adding only texture to the soup, which is flavored by spices and chicken or pork broth. Other health-related industries have fostered public belief in shark fins having medicinal qualities. What was once reserved for royalty as it was believed to bring strength and virility, is now known to do nothing positive for disease or health whatsoever.

Despite the fins doing nothing beneficial, the word is out that fins mean money. Even the most decrepit boats can turn huge profits as expensive refrigeration systems aren't needed as they would be if the entire shark body was kept for other uses.

Currently, 16 countries have banned shark finning but enforcement in these areas remains a problem. Despite being banned, many countries' regulations are incredibly loose. Finners can circumvent the law by removing the fins from the sharks before being brought to port.

The heart of the issue behind decimating shark populations lies in the

A destroyed coral reef.
Reefs are often bombed using homemade explosives created with diesel fuel and fertilizer. The bombs immobilize the fish, and destroy the ecosystems, which take hundreds and often thousands of years to build. Cyanide fishing also destroys reefs. Fishermen seeking tropical fish for the pet trade squirt cyanide inside reefs, which immobilizes or kills the fish, while killing the coral. Some of the fish are only immobilized, and later recover, and these are sold into the tropical fish trade.

demand. Surveys on the ground in China show that three-quarters of respondents don't know where shark fins come from or how they are gathered. Interestingly, the translation of shark fin soup in Chinese doesn't contain the word "shark."

Promoting awareness about the issue will have an effect. If the public was made aware that 95 percent of the meat from finned sharks for the soup they consume is discarded, that shark populations have declined 90 percent because of overfishing, and that sharks are incredibly important to the health of the oceans and the planet, I believe that demand would wane.

Sharks also suffer from a crisis of perception. Conservation is not high on the list when sharks are portrayed as menacing people killers, a myth largely perpetuated by the media. After all, dangerous sharks sell more newspapers, draw more eyeballs to the TV screens, and create great material for the entertainment industry. Championing sharks is often like championing the plague, so despite their ecological importance, the public often turns its head and supports conservation efforts for the cute and cuddly animals.

My mission is to educate people and help them see sharks not as the dangerous man-eaters they've been portrayed as, but as incredibly important animals that want little to do with people. Whales were once seen as sea monsters. Captain Ahab's Moby Dick was a man hunter. Over time, public opinion changed—people discovered that whales were in danger of extinction, and because of public pressure, the International Whaling Commission was formed, and whales were saved. A similar thing can happen with sharks. Any social change in the past has been carried out by a small percentage of the planet. Humans have evolved in the past towards cultural, racial and gender equality. We can evolve to save sharks. All that's needed is pressure from the public, and governments and corporations will respond.

We've spent the last few thousand years building a sophisticated global economy at the expense of the natural world. It's time to change our economic models, time to shift our focus toward making money, generating jobs, and helping the economy by designing life, systems and tools that work in harmony with the natural world, not against it.

There is simply no issue more important. Conservation is the preservation of human life on earth, and that, above all else, is worth fighting for.

A fishing net that was caught on a coral reef, Sabah, Malaysia. Fishing nets are often made of synthetic material that does not biodegrade. These nets can float in the ocean for decades, ensnaring animals and fish. Predators are attracted to the dead and dying fish and these predators and scavengers are often caught in the net as well. The dead animals eventually rot and fall off, while the nets continue to trap ocean creatures.

Small net fishing on the Mekong River, Vietnam. Fishing on this scale can be sustainable, but increasing technology such as huge factory ships is clearing the oceans of fish, while wasting much of their catch. Every single fishery is expected to have totally collapsed by 2048, a sign that our relationship with the oceans is not working.

Galápagos shark with a hook in its mouth and damaged dorsal fin from entanglement in longlines. I photographed this female the day after we cut hundreds of sharks off illegally set longlines at Darwin Island, Galápagos Islands, Ecuador.

Hooks used by long-liners are huge, and difficult to remove because of their barbs. Longlines can have more than 16,000 baited hooks that catch and kill sharks, billfish, tunas, seabirds, sea lions, and sea turtles.

Crown-of-thorns starfish consuming plate coral, Great Barrier Reef, Australia. Destruction of coral reefs is destroying the habitat for many shark species.

Abandoned fish traps, Coral Sea, Australia. The oceans are often seen as our waste dump. Until the ban on dumping plastics from ships and other vessels, 16 billion pounds of plastics were dumped into the ocean annually.

Shark fishermen, Mantanani Island, Sabah, Malaysian Borneo. Many traditional cultures along coasts have fished and relied on sharks for centuries. Many of these traditional fisheries are now threatened by large-scale industrialized fishing. These fishermen sell their fins to a local trader, and keep the bodies to feed their families.

22" SHARK JAW
$199.99
SKU 241680

HAND C
BAMBOO

Shark jaws are often sold as curios to tourists. Supporting the sale of shark parts, even though the animal is already dead, creates and fuels the demand for shark parts, damaging shark populations that are already severely depleted.

This shop in Key West, Florida, had hundreds of shark jaws for sale. Many of these sharks were killed just for their jaws and fins. Shark meat is often thought of as cheap meat, so it is often renamed as flake, rock salmon, or other types of fish to disguise it, and mislead consumers. Much of the fish-and-chips market is "flake" or spiny dogfish, which is a shark that can live to be 150 years old.

The teeth from the endangered great white shark for sale in Key West, Florida. The purchase of white teeth supports often unsustainable and illegal shark fishing. If you like shark teeth, purchase fossilized teeth that are often grey or brown.

Shark fins drying on the roof of a shark finning boat, Sabah, Malaysian Borneo. Even the most decrepit boats can fin for sharks because the fins are dried, and don't need the expensive refrigeration systems that whole bodies or fish meat needs.

Baby sharks for sale in a market in Singapore. Sharks have been fished so extensively that even baby sharks are found for sale in markets. Their fins will most likely be sold separately.

FACING PAGE: **A juvenile shark having its fins cut off in a Malaysian market.** The bodies of small sharks are more often kept for food because large sharks have high concentrations of uric acid in their flesh, and spoil quickly.

Shark fin is advertised in stores and restaurants because of its association with wealth. It has become a staple at weddings, banquets, and business dinners. More than three-quarters of respondents in a survey conducted by WildAid in China don't know where shark fin came from or how it was gathered. The Chinese word for shark fin means "fish wing."

A landing dock at a market in Malaysia, full of sharks and rays. There are few regulations at all regarding sharks, and many fishermen can't tell the difference between one species and another, making it difficult to impose quotas or regulations on a single species despite drastic declines. There are no international regulations to protect sharks.

A whale or basking shark fin on display at a shark fin soup restaurant in Bangkok, Thailand. The large fins are a huge draw for consumers, and restaurants will pay tens of thousands of dollars for large fins like this, putting pressure on the slow-moving, easy-to-catch, and endangered filter feeders.

The sizes of the average sharks landed have declined dramatically over the last 30 years. Most of the mature animals have been caught, and now many are killed before reproductive maturity, which damages populations greatly. Most of the sharks that turn up at markets in Asia are now quite small.

EVERY 90 MINUTES, MORE THAN 15,000 SHARKS ARE KILLED.

DUE TO PUBLIC PRESSURE TO PROTECT SHARKS, LONG-LINING IN
THE GALÁPAGOS IS NOW ILLEGAL.

COSTA RICANS CONTINUE TO FIGHT AGAINST SHARK FINNING.

24 COUNTRIES INCLUDING AMERICAN SAMOA, AUSTRALIA, BRAZIL,
CAPE VERDE, CANADA, COLUMBIA, COSTA RICA, ECUADOR, EGYPT,
EL SALVADOR, THE EUROPEAN UNION, FRENCH POLYNESIA, ISRAEL, MALTA,
MEXICO, NAMIBIA, NICARAGUA, NEW ZEALAND, OMAN, PALAU, PANAMA,
THE PHILIPPINES, SOUTH AFRICA AND THE UNITED STATES
HAVE BANNED SHARK FINNING.

VISIT WWW.SAVINGSHARKS.COM FOR MORE INFORMATION.